THE SYMBOLIC TENDENCY IN IRISH RENAISSANCE

By

Dr. K. C. BHATNAGAR, M.A., Ph.D.
S. D. COLLEGE, MUZAFFARNAGAR (U.P.)

FOLCROFT LIBRARY EDITIONS / 1974

The Symbolic Tendency in Irish Renaissance

THE IRISH mind—like the Indian—is fundamentally lyrical and goes for things distant and 'eerie', exotic and supernatural. The symbolic tendency was, on the whole, a reaction against the early naturalistic drama of Ibsen, Shaw and Galsworthy. Strangely enough, Ibsen in his *The Wild Duck*, Shaw in his *Heartbreak House* and Galsworthy in *The Pigeon* developed the symbolic tendency—thus proving that mere naturalism was not enough. Further, Maeterlinck with his *The Blue Bird* and Tchekov with his *The Cherry Orchard* accentuated the symbolic tendency. In France particularly, Stephen Mallarme in his poetry spotlighted the life of sensations and emotions as against the life of reason and intellect. W. B. Yeats who was the spearhead of the Irish Renaissance wrote clearly about his indebtedness to the French Symboliste tradition :—

> "The mystical life is the centre of all I do and all that I think and all that I write...I have always considered myself a voice of what I consider to be a great renaissance the revolt of the soul against the intellect—now beginning in the world."[1]

The rapid advance of Science could not take away from Yeats's love of mysticism and symbolism. Wagner's dramas, Keat's Odes and Mallarme's poetry struck at the root of 18th century rationalism and 19th century materialism. In later life, Yeats registered an advance from the earlier medieval mystic images of the Pre-Raphaelites : the palm, the wreath, the Lily and the dove. He became, like Blake, a systematic mystic who not only delighted in a traditional symbolism but evolved a personal symbolism of his own ; linking up dream with reality. One symbol to which Yeats returns again and again is "Sligo"—his spiritual home to which also belongs the Lake Isle of Innisfree—a symbol which exercised an irresistible charm over his imagination whenever he was placed in the vortex of modern civilisation. His Byzantine poems reveal a rare sense-versus-spirit conflict :—

> Consume my heart away ; sick with desire
> And fastened to a dying animal
> It knows not what it is ; and gather me
> Into the artifice of eternity.
> —*Sailing To Byzantium.*

---

1. Divided Image : Margaret Rudd (Routledge and Kegan Paul) P. 58 Quoted from Ellman, The Man and the Masks.

Symbolism of a rare type shines out through the later poems of Yeats. It even establishes contact with the Indian Philosophy. It is the symbolism of the Self and the Anti-Self: the first representing the social self and the second, the higher one. In the poem: *Ego, Dominus Tuus*, Hic who symbolizes the religious man chides Ille for his magical obsessions :—

> On the grey sand beside the shallow stream,
> Under your old wind-beaten tower......
> You walk in the moon,
> And although you have passed the best of life, still trace
> Enthralled by the unconquerable delusion,
> Magical shapes.

Yeats confirms the view that the Anti-Self rouses the Self to reach new heights of spiritualism :—

> "The anti-self is the Mask—a being in all things opposite to the natural state, an image of desire, an image symbolical of that state of mind which is of all states of mind not impossible, the most difficult—because only the greatest obstacle that can be contemplated without despair, rouses the will to full intensity."[2]

Magic and music deepen the Celtic twilight and make it a fitting background for the fairy world of the Irish Renaissance. The Irish drama may lack an elaborate structure; but it is steeped in subtle and suggestive symbolism. Yeats who, with the help of Lady Gregory, founded the Irish National Theatre in 1901 found in Irish mythology "so much of a new beauty that it may well give the opening century its most memorable symbols." Symbolism thus becomes the central fact of the Irish Renaissance.[3] The figures of the Irish drama step in and out of the stage in a faint, far-off manner; yet they can hardly be called puppets or marionettes. They are not touched by the Russian sense of bitterness and brooding fatalism. They either become symbols of an

---

2. W. B. Yeats : Autobiography, P. 170.

3. Wagner had already prepared the ground for this switch-over to symbolism through his opera in London and Paris (1855-60) with Stephen Mallarme who only echoed Wagner when he said :

> "The plasticity of a symbol was to correspond to sculpture ; the illusionism of a symbol was to correspond to Painting ; the final end of Poetry was to be music, because it was music and not poetry that contained the most perfect abstraction."
>
> (Stephen Mallarme : Hayse Coopermann : Columbia ; P. 99.)

idea or an inner spiritual reality. In Yeats's *Cathleen Ni Houlihan* (1902), the old crone who seduces Michael from his fiancée on the eve of their wedding assumes the character of rejuvenated Ireland ; Michael's mother questions her younger son : "Did you see an old woman going down the path ?" "I did not" answers the kid, "but I saw a young girl and she had the walk of queen."

Yeats's *The Hour Glass* (1903) rests on a symbolism of the type of Morality play, wherein knowledge in the person of the Wise Man is pitted against Blind Faith in the person of the Fool—to decide the issue of human salvation. The theme is further elaborated in Yeats's *Where There Is Nothing* (1904). Herein a wealthy gentleman Paul Ruttledge turns tinker, monk and mystic. Finally he gets out of time into eternity. One by one, he puts out seven altar candles : symbolizing Laws, Towns, the Church, Hope, Memory, Thought and the Sun. Where there is NOTHING, there is God. Paul concludes ; "We have learned too much ; our minds are like troubled water—we get nothing but broken images." In plays like this, the stress is shifted from dramatic illusion to transference of emotion, mood and atmosphere. The theatre seems to have left realism behind and developed a distinctly symbolic tendency.

Yeats's later plays : *Four Plays for Dancers* (1920) are modelled on the Japanese Nō Plays, even though F. R. Higgins would claim them as "bloodless relations to the elaborate masques of the Elizabethan days."[4] The Nō Plays of Japan were translated in 1913 and were, according to Professor Noguchi, "Trees rising from the rich soil of tradition and Buddhistic faith"..............at the end of each play, a priest conducts by meditation and prayer : "the ghost of a warrior, a lady, a flower or a tree into the blessings of Nirvana."[5] Chorus, dance, music and mask : are some of the Nō features adopted by Yeats. He has, like Gordon Craig, revolted against the gaudy trappings of a picture-frame stage to give the fullest possible scope to a symbolic setting. The attention of a spectator in the Nō Play has to be dynamic ; the mind has to be liberated from all technical inhibitions—by special strains of an orchestra consisting of a flute, a harp, a drum and a gong. Says Arthur Walley :

"Forget the theatre and look at the Nō (=talent) ; forget the Nō and look at the actor. Forget the actor and look at the idea

---

4. L. Robinson : The Irish Theatre ; Macmillan 1939 P. 84.
5. While lecturing to the Calcutta University, 1936.

('kokore' in Japanese). Forget the idea and you will understand the Nō."[6]

Music and poetry get fused together in this context; there is no action worth the name; but there is a feeling of suspense intensified by a frozen dance—to give resonance to which large earthen pots are buried underground. In such a dance-drama, "the rhythms of motion, mood, music and movement unite in one supercharged symbol."[7]

The stress shifts from a matter-of-fact representation to a presentational immediacy. Yeats could not however, expect a select chamber audience as the Japanese playwrights could do. The actor with the mask on became an abstract symbol—not a dynamic reality on the stage. He had to adjust his acting to the time of the performance. On the whole, the Nō technique with its masks, symbolic properties and a nominal action accompanied by music and dance gave Yeats ample opportunity to practise the various stages in the structure of a Nō-Play :—

1. *Yūgen* (Lit. that lies beneath the surface) which is applied to the natural grace of a boy's movement. (The Japanese drama has been anti-feminist since the Kabuki period down to 1900). Yūgen moreover, is a vocal movement in quietude and quietude in movement or the realisation of a state of identity in which the art and the teachings of Zen are "perfectly harmonised."[8]

2. Besides Yūgen in the Nō, there is *Yukyo* (Lit. to play as far as madness).

3. *Kurai* (Lit. an emotional quality or atmosphere.)

4. *Ban-i* (Lit. the free expression of spirit).

This synthetic technique aimed at the unification of human sensibility. How far Yeats has been able to achieve this objective in his later Plays —is yet an open question. The sheer lyricism of the Nō Plays suggests primitive emotions, images and rhythms and hearkens back to fairy-

---

6. Nō Plays of Japan (Introduction). The Japanese Book Criticism.

7. E. Drew : Discovering Drama : P. 219. Cf. Arthur Walley :

   "The piercing Nō flute intervenes at the beginning. at the climax and the end. The hypnotic effect of drum taps is well-known. The drummers have the nerves of the audience in their hands. By a sudden accelerando, they can create an atmosphere of almost unendurable tension."

8. Foreword by Iwao Kongo : Nogaku : Beatrice L. Suzuki : Lond.

tales, folk-lore and legends.[9] Further, it ventures forth to experiment with the verbal medium towards the direction of pure poetry and occultism. Yeats grew so enamoured of the Japanese Nō Play that he enlisted the services of a Japanese dancer in the performance of his own plays. Yeats however, could not touch the excellence of speech cadences and musical stresses in the Nō Plays ; but he did imbibe their esoteric atmosphere and half-mythological background. Passages such as the following from *The Dreaming of the Bones* (1919) (Song for the folding and unfolding of the cloth) leave us absolutely cold :

> First Musician (Or all three Musicians, singing)
> Why does my heart beat so ?
> Did not a shadow pass ?
> It passed but a moment ago,
> Who can have trod in the grass ?
> What rogue is night-wandering ?
> Have not old writers said
> That dizzy dreams can spring
> From the dry bones of dead ?

In the last 20 years of his life from *The Wild Swans at Coole* ('19) to the posthumous *Last Poems and Plays* ('39), Yeats turns into a symbolist-realist : thus proving that the real anti-thesis of symbolism is not realism but naturalism. In the last thing, Yeats was working *The Death of Cuchulain*, an eternal harlot speaks of physical passion, the fear and delight of the battle, the gods and heroes who inspire us at critical moments with a realism which is striking :—

> That there are still some living
> That my limbs unclothe,
> But that the flesh my flesh has gripped
> I both adore and loathe.
> (Pipe and drum music).[10]

All this a far cry from the symbolism of his earlier poems and plays. Symbolism in the Irish Renaissance seems to have a living structure. The Irish drama, poetry, folk-lore and mythology seem to be steeped in it. Very often the symbols used by the Irish writers don't merely represent the general idea or a dream image—but get across and become a living revelation of the mysterious and the inscrutable. To that

---

9. A. Nicoll thinks that the Symbolic Drama has developed into three directions ; 1. The Supernatural and the Fairy World. 2. Historical Themes. 3. Poetic treatment of real life. (British Drama VI) Yeats's main contribution lies in the first direction.

10. Quoted : G. S. Fraser ; W. B. Yeats : The British Council : P. 24. (1958)

extent the Irish drama may be termed an example of transcendental symbolism. But then symbolism in the Irish drama has an organic structure : taking its humble origin in the first fine rapture of Yeats's early poems and plays, reaching ripeness in the dramas of J. M. Synge (1871-1909) and then sliding into senile decay in the half-satirical and half-allegorical dramas of Sean O' Casey (B. 1884). The note of Celtic symbolism is heard time and again from the Arthurian Legends to writers like Blake and Shelley. The Moscow Art Theatre founded in 1898 by Stanislavsky was another attempt to reflect the emotional upsurge of a people—trying to create a new social order. In this case, however, the theatre became a national force greater than the Irish Theatre and even transcended the personality of the dramatist. In The Moscow Art Theatre, the actor *ispo facto* became the Tribune or the leader of men ; the stage setting became purely symbolic and renounced all archeological and spectacular appeal. A similar movement was seen in the English Theatre. Gordon Craig sought to synthesise the simple essentials of a play through design backed by colour ; whereas Appia went forth to fuse his actors and setting in light.[11] This however, led to the emergence of Expressionism on the English stage. In place of a backdrop, wings and solid plastic setting, the theatre artists began painting in forms which may be called 'cubist', 'futurist' or 'expressionist.' In any case the theatre passed from naturalism to symbolism. The theatre according to Macgowan,[12] developed a third dimension based on a "sculpturesque lighting," to which may also be added a fourth dimension : the relationship of drama with life in general, a philosophy propounded by the Chorus as in the Greek drama or the Japanese Nō drama. The Irish dramatists were primarily not men of theatre ; but as William Archer points out :—"The history of Irish undertaking shows how a little seed of sacrifice, sown in fertile soil, may bring forth an almost miraculous harvest."[13]

Synge was discovered by Yeats in Paris, when both were slowly coming under the influence of the French Symbolistes. His dramatic appeal is greater than that of Yeats chiefly because he caught the speech rhythms of the peasant girls of the Aran Islands. Synge has justly been compared to Shakespeare—only like that of Marlowe, his

---

11. Craig produced Hamlet at the Moscow Art Theatre in 1912 by folding screens to suit the various scenes of the play. The stage, as a result of this innovation, ceased to represent objects but began to present emotion.

12. The Theatre of Tomorrow.

13. The Old Drama and the New : New York (1929) P. 369.

career was cut short in its prime. He is equally good at Comedy, Folk-history and Tragedy. "The measure of his excellence is the measure of the excellence of the whole movement."[14] Yet Synge could not rise above peasant life to give us the morally idealistic figure of a lady like Masefield's *Nan*. He evolved however, an Anglo-Irish dialect which remains supreme in its simplicity and suggestiveness even to this day. Throughout his dramas, there runs a deep strain of nature symbolism which for its sincerity can only be compared with Wordsworth's nature pantheism. He reaches out to the primitive sources of Irish culture and tradition. In *Riders to the Sea* (1904) for instance, the sea becomes the omnivorous villain for the entire family of Maurya, a tragic heroine after the Greek model.[15] The Sea becomes a malicious agent of the inscrutable working out the ruin of an entire family and is not appeased till Maurya cries out in utter resignation :

> "They're all gone now, and there isn't anything more the Sea can do to me...... It is a great rest I'll have now......"

Greek simplicity has been wedded to French subtlety ; the play is a simple and spontaneous symphony—pervasive and yet organic. Yeats on his first reading of this play exclaimed : "Aeschylus !" and then after a moment's pause : "No, Sophocles !" Maurya is deluded by the vision of dead Michael "riding a gray pony........with fine clothes on him and new shoes on his feet." This vision symbolized for the already bereft mother the doom also of her sixth child. It is drama stripped to the bone ; there is hardly any attempt at dramatic structure or motivation of events.

In *The Playboy of the Western World* (1907), we have the figure of a mock parricide who thinks he has murdered his father but has not, in reality, done so. He however, arouses the sense of hero-worship in Shawn's fiancée-Pegeen Flaherty and a bevy of other village girls. The so-called "murdered" father stages a come-back to the utter discomfiture of the "parricide" Christy Mahon, who again tries to repeat his attack on the father ; but is handed over to the Police (the Peelers) for all

14. F. W. Chandler : Aspects of Modern Drama · Macmillan ; (1929) P. 275.

15. In Synge's hands, even prose becomes poetry : There is no conscious attempt at symbolism ; yet the play challenges comparison with *King Lear* in passages like this ;—(Maurya, the universal mother bereft of her children speaks) :

> "Michael has a clean burial in the far north, by the grace of the Almighty God. Bartley will have a fine coffin out of the white boards, and a deep grave surely. What more can we want than that ? No man at all can be living for ever, and we must be satisfied."

his pains. Christy has been interpreted by critics as the Spirit of Drama and as a symbol of the Oedipus Complex. In the Preface to the Play, Synge has explained his position clearly :

> "On the stage one must have reality and one must have joy and that is why the intellectual modern drama has failed and people have grown sick of the false joy of the musical comedy......"

In the Shadow of the Glen (1903) brings into relief the morality of an Irish peasant woman which Ireland has even kept sacrosant as if in a case of rose-tinted glass. The play is a typically Syngesque combination of realism and symbolism. Unlike Russia, in Ireland morality—being a fixed thing—cannot be questioned. So when the heroine of the play Nora—being tired of leading a dull life-decides to elope with a tramp in the presence of her old hubby, the Roman Catholic Irish peasantry was naturally offended. Professor Corkery finds in Synge's Nora "a woman who wears her lusts on her sleeve." In any case she is a dull copy of Nora the heroine of Ibsen's *Doll's House*, who at least becomes the centre of an emotional crisis, sustains our interest till the end and even flings a surprise on us by not being reconciled to her husband but by telling him: "Sit down by Torvald you and I have much to say to each other." The tramp in the play uses a musical and pictorial language which has a cadence all its own :—

> "We'll be going now, I'm telling you, and the time you'll be feeling the cold and the frost and the frost and the great rain and the sun again and the south wind blowing in the glens, you'll not be sitting up on a wet ditch...... Making yourself old with looking on each day, and it passing you by."

The symbolism of *The Well of the Saints* (1905) is however, tinctured with cynicism. Herein a beggar and his wife—both blind—are gifted with sight with the well-water by the Saint. Both had thought each other to be beautiful but the stark-naked reality of their withered visages repels them so much that they quarrel and when the Saint offers to cure them of their blindness once again, the old beggar throws down the goblet of blessed water—proving thereby that the world of illusion is better than the world of reality.

The dramatic efforts of Yeats and Synge enriched the modern poetic drama in several ways. Like the Irish pioneers, the modern poetic dramatists started looking for inspiration in the ancient legends and sagas, maidens and the moonlight, thunder and the sea, angels and the devils-lions and the lambs, doves and nightingales. Dr. Gordon better than the Bottomley took his cue from the Irish dramatists when he related dramatic poetry to contemporary folk-speech :—

> "I think that if poetry is to regain its right of entry to the theatre, it must learn to base itself upon contemporary speech rhythms, though not necessarily speech-usages, upon contemporary sound and not either the look of a printed page or a bygone usage of sound.[16]

As against the above assertion, it may well be urged that T. S. Eliot in our own times has not based his drama on living speech rhythms but has often reverted to past liturgy, anti-phonal use of Choric speech and Early Morality technique to provide us relief from the present crisis of faith.

In *Deirdre of the Sorrows* (1910) Synge takes up a legendary theme already used by Yeats three years earlier. The action thus, is predetermined. It is only in characterisation and diction that we find traces of symbolism. Deirdre, for instance speaks of "waking with the smell of June in the tops of grasses" and of having been "one time the like of a ewe looking for a lamb that had been taken away from her, and one time seeing new gold on the stars, and a new face on the moon." The whole play is full of a symbolic imagery calculated to intensify the "feeling content" of the play.

Although an Irish dramatist, Lord Dunsany (1878-1958) looked not to Ireland but to the Orient for inspiration. It is a world of fear, terror and revenge into which we are ushered. In *A Night at an Inn* (1916), the Toff and his three followers have stolen a precious jewel from the eye of an Eastern idol, but are tracked down to England by the three priests. The Toff is successful in luring the priests away to a deserted spot and killing them. But then, the Nemesis falls upon the Toff as the Idol enters—groping like a blind man—for the ruby and then moving off with it. Then a voice is heard from outside calling the miscreants—one by one—a voice which they dare not disobey. Death is the punishment they receive. The Toff is constrained to say : "I did not foresee it." It is a rare synthesis of Oriental religion and Occidental materialism—giving rise to a macabre setting.[17] Symbolism triumphs again in Dunsany's *The Gods of the Mountain* (1911). Some

---

16. Quoted : Times Literary Supplement : Jan 24, 1935.

17. The play may well be taken to symbolize the revenge of the Spiritual world on the Material ; the foreboding grows into a palpitating fear ; there is a spell of silence before the final date with Death ; the suspense rises to a climax in Toff's remark : "*I did not foresee it.*"

beggars who impose themselves on a superstitious people are turned to stone. In Agmar, Dunsany has tried to symbolize the eternal aspiration of man to reach a state of godhood.

> *Agmar* :   Is not all life a beggary to the gods ?
> Do they not see all men always begging of them and asking alms, with incense and bells and subtle devices ?

He deludes himself into thinking that he is the "oldest of divinities" ; and refuses to partake of the flesh offered to the other "gods of the mountain" : beggars other than himself. He spills even the "Woldery" wine offered to him by the citizens. Yet when they are gone, he eats hungrily on the sly. When a citizen requests him to resurrect his dead child, this self-styled god retorts by dubbing death itself as the "child of gods" ! Even after such rebuffs, the people cannot help suffering from a guilty conscience :—

> "We have doubted them ; they have turned to stone because we have doubted them......they were true gods."

Dunsany's *Tents of the Arabs* (1920) symbolizes in the person of a king, the lure of a nomadic life. The king abdicates his throne and follows the caravans on their way to Holy Mecca. He has a romance with a gipsy girl-Eznarza ; and their love-prattle recalls the measured cadence of Syngesque prose :—

> *King*: We shall hear the nomads stirring in their camps far off, because it is dawn.
>
> *Eznarza* : The jackals will patter past us slipping back to the hills.
>
> *King* : When at the evening, the sun is set we shall weep for no day that is gone.
>
> *Eznarza* : I will rise up my head of a night time against the sky, and the old unbought stars shall twinkle through my hair and we shall not envy any of the diademed queens of the world.

The lovers have leapt over logic and reached the state of intuition which prepares the ground for symbolism.

The Flight of the Queen portrays the flight of the Queen Bee : a theme also exploited by Maeterlinck. The drama in the insect world is well-nigh translated into human terms,—no attempt being made to point a moral or teach in parables—a bane of the Irish dramatists. Even the names of the bees are deliciously symbolical. The Prince of Zoon, Prince Meliflor, Queen Zoomzoomarma and the Overlord of

Moomoomon. Love forms the subject of a controversy in the Bee-world :—

> *Queen* : Love is a joy, Oozizi ; love is a glow. Love makes them dance so lightly along rays of sunlight. ......It is like flowers in twilight. How should they sigh ?
>
> *Oozizi* : Lady, Great Lady. Say not such things of love.
>
> *Queen* : My mother love, Oozizi.
>
> *Oozizi* : Lady, for a day. For one day, mighty lady. As one might stoop in idleness to a broken toy and pick it up and throw it again away ; so she loved for a day. That idle fancy of an afternoon tarnished no pinnacle that shone from her exalted station.

In the meantime, the call—sudden and irresistible—comes from the Aether mountain—the call of Prince Zoon who ventures forth to kiss the hand of the Queen-Bee only to meet his doom with the last word "Zoomzoomarma" on his lips.

Edward Martyn (1859-1923) represents the later phase of Ibsen, the Ibsen of *The Wild Duck* and *The Lady From The Sea*—rather than *The Doll's House*. His two plays : *The Heather Field* (1899) and *Maeve* (1900) are supreme examples of an Ibsenseque symbolism, in which the Irish National Theatre establishes contact with the Scandinavian.

The Heather Field is a 3-act play. It depicts the tragedy of an idealist—Carden Tyrrell, who much against the wishes of his wife wants to sacrifice his worldy ambitions to reclaim and improve the Heather Field which symbolizes Ireland herself. His wife's attempt to have Tyrrell declared insane by a doctor falls through because of the timely intervention of Barry Ussher. The reclamation of the waste-land is pursued by Tyrrell even at the cost of mortgages and debts. He evicts his tenants which leads to Agrarian trouble. Tyrrell has to move about under a police escort, an idea which he abhors like all true idealists. At long last, the barren and rocky heather field blossoms forth—thus symbolizing Tyrrell's desires. But lo ! the pasturage is relapsing into wilderness—which gives Tyrrell the greatest shock of his life. The *leit motive* of the play recalls Ibsen's *The Wild Duck*, while the closing scene reads like Ibsen's *Ghosts*. Tyrrell begins to address his son Kit (who has plucked a bunch of heather) as his younger brother :—

> See, even now the sky is darkening as in that storm scene of the old legend I told you on the Rhine. See the rain across the saffron sun trembles like gold harp—strings, through the purple Irish spring.

And then as the father and the son watch the rainbow, he bursts out:

> Oh, mystic highway of man's speechless longings, my heart goes forth upon the rainbow to that horizon of joy……

The dialogue takes on a Syngesque colour; symbolism becomes pervasive. So ends the age-old struggle between man and nature ; so did it end in Synge's *Riders to the Sea*.

In *Maeve* (1900)—a 2-act play—there is again a clash between the ideal and the practical angle on life. Maeve O' Heynes is torn between her love of Ireland and love of ideal beauty. Her father and sister commit her to marriage with a rich Englishman. But her nurse is convinced that Maeve is no other than the metamorphosed Queen Maeve of the Irish legend. When Maeve is asked by the nurse to visit the Queen and her lover (symbol of eternal beauty) in the fairyland, Maeve is found cold and lifeless—her soul having departed for the world beyond. No wonder, both Yeats and George Moore found in Maeve "the spirit and sense of an ill-fated race"—a tragedy-of-Ireland symbolism.

Martyn did not get a square deal at the Irish Theatre ; so he developed a satirical vein which mars much of symbolism in *The Enchanted Sea (produced 1902)*. It is a play modelled on Ibsen's *Lady From The Sea*. Guy Font, a young squire is reported to have "fairy-blood in his vein" being possessed by the Sea-Spirit. Being drowned through his aunt's machinations, he is made to enter symbolically into an elemental life, the life of the Sea. The aunt quits the stage by committing suicide ; but the crude realism of the play is partially relieved by the imaginative "Lord Mask".

Symbolism is fighting for a last stand in *Grangecolman* (1912). There is a negative Chekovian atmosphere in the play. Disillusionment strikes the key-note of the play. Clara Farquhar shoots down Catherine ; but all this is accidental, not symbolical. Martyn does not have the stature of Yeats and Synge ; but with his blend of realism and symbolism he has put the Irish Renaissance on the literary map of Europe.

Lennox Robinson (B. 1886) in most of his early dramas is concerned with domestic life, family pride etc., pitted against love of Ireland.

In *The Patriots* (1912), we see the discomfiture of an old Irish revolutionary—James Nugent at the hands of an audience which has left to see the latest film in utter disregard of his earlier eloquence. We see in the play a cynical strain corroding any suggestion there might be of symbolism.

In *The Lost Leader* (1918), there are a few traces of symbolism. It is based on an Irish legend that the Uncrowned King of Ireland, Charles Stewart Parnell (who died in 1891 ?) is still alive. The scene is a fishing hotel run by Mary and her uncle—Lucius Lenihan. The latter is supposed to be "Parnell" by the psychiatrist, Power Harper who passes on the idea to his friend Frank Ormsby in the smoking room of the hotel. While the psychiatrist is trying to hypnotise a roaming journalist-Augustus Smith, Lucius enters and sits at a distance unnoticed by the party, and gets hypnotised into the bargain. The patient "Parnell" now refers to his dreams of 20 years ago : a coffin, a woman, false friends and his own name ! The doctor puts these dreams—one by one—into his cigar box—each dream counting for one cigar—and means to drop them into the lake for ever. The patient Parnell now assumes the role of a "real" Parnell. He promises to bring proofs of his "identity" on a mountain summit. The half-comic political party squabbles that follow hardly symbolize the internal strife of Ireland.

In the '*mêlée*', a blind man of the mob strikes Parnell fatally. Parnell's friends who arrive at the scene can only vouchsafe that there is a similarity of features between "this" Parnell and "that" Parnell. We may say that in this play, there is a complete illusionment of the audience even though there is no inherent belief in the symbolism adduced—even though A. E. Morgan considers that Parnell's sudden death :

"On the symbolical plane may be justified as truly tragic ; Ireland's strife inevitably destroys her Lost Leader."[18]

In *John Ferguson* (1915) of St. John Greer Ervine (B. 1883) we have the hero Ferguson symbolizing the rigid protestantism of Ulster. A willing martyr to misfortunes, his daughter Hannah is raped by Witherow to whom his fame too is mortgaged. A rival suitor of Hannah—James Ceasar is reported to have killed Witherow, even though Ceaser confesses that courage failed him in his attempt to murder Witherow. Ferguson goes out to save the soul of the supposed murderer from damnation. Later on, it transpires that Hannah's brother Andrew is the real murderer of Witherow, John lets Andrew confess his crime to the Police and reads the Bible to his broken wife ; thus proving—what has been proved times out of number—that nothing

---

18. Tendencies In Modern English Drama (1924) p. 221.

can destroy the invincible soul of man. The figure of Ferguson becomes symbolical of human faith which moves mountains and does not lapse into a poised utterance as most of the figures of Shaw's earlier plays do.

Sean O' Casey has been noted by J. W. Cunliffe as the greatest Irish discovery since the War, not only of the Abbey Theatre but also of the European drama[19]. With him Irish drama reaches its last phase—of decay ; and enters into two new fields : photographic realism and expressionism.

The Dublin slums provide the background for Casey's tragicomedy : *Juno and the Paycock* (1924). The plot emanates out of the Civil War between the New Free State and the Republicans in 1922 which brought disaster to many Irish homes. The atmosphere becomes negative in the extreme. Captain Jack Boyle is the author's greatest realistic creation[20]. A Porter's family lives under the illusion of an imaginary fortune settled on it. The drunken porter has the worst of it in the end when he returns home only to come up against the death of his son, the flight to the river of his forsaken and pregnant daughter and the desertion of Juno, his wife. It is something more than realism can do.

The Silver Tassie (1929) is a whole night 4-act drama of war with a pacifist approach. The Silver Tassie (a football cup) ripens into a symbol of Harry Heegan's love for Jessie, when he drinks her health in this cup on the eve of his departure for War front. The soldiers on the Western front speak (like the Chorus in the Greek Drama) of the different aspects of war. There is a strange blend of realism and expressionism : the one dovetailing into other. Harry has been crippled in war and Jessie has in the meantime accepted another lover : Barney. The dialogue of the soldiers is full of expressionism :—

1st Soldier : Cold and wet and tir'd.
2nd Soldier : Wet and tir'd and cold.
3rd Soldier : Tir'd and cold and wet.
4th Soldier : Twelve blasted hours of ammunition transport fatigue !

19. Modern English Playwrights : Harper.
20 O'Casey can concentrate on the painful life of the people already doomed to failure with as great verisimilitude as Chekov. Captain Boyle's final remark :
"I am telling you...Joxer th' whole world's in a terrible state of chassis"...
is certainly more than pathetic.

1st Soldier : Twelve weary hours.
2nd Soldier : And wasting hours.
3rd Soldier : And hot and heavy hours.
1st Soldier : Toiling and thinking to build the wall of force that blocks the way from here to home.

In the third act, at the hospital, we see Harry being wheeled about in an invalid chair, the quarrelsome husband Teddy now war-blind, Barney, war-wounded, Susie, (who once loved Harry) now in love with Surgeon Maxwell. The last act shifts to the dance hall of the Avondale Football Club. Teddy falls into a sympathetic communion with Harry as they see the others dancing. Their innermost feelings are "expressed" through short, cryptic sentences

Harry : I never felt the hand that made me helpless.
Teddy : I never saw the hand that made me blind.
Harry : Life came and took away the half of life.
Teddy : Life took from me the half he left with you.
Harry : The Lord hath given and the Lord hath taken away.
Teddy : Blessed be the name of the Lord.

Barney being surprised in his love-talk with Jessie, tries to kill Harry but cannot do so because the friends intervene. Silver Tassie has now become a symbol of love that is no more. Harry leaves it to Barney and Jessie. Susie strikes a note that is echoed by all lovers :—

> He is gone, we remain and so
> Let him wrap himself up in his woe—
> For he is a life on the ebb,
> We, a full life on the flow.

Thus laughter and tears lie cheek by jowl in this play. The dialogue consists of patterned phrases, allusions and external symbols but lacks logic.

> "Instead, as if the drama were being rolled over and tossed in air before our eyes like a diamond we are so to observe its facets of tragedy, comedy and open farce that their flashing becomes at last one flash and perhaps by imaginative and symbolic transition, one spiritual light."[21]

Within the Gates (1934) presents in an expressionist manner shadowy figures (not types) chosen at random : a bishop, a whore, a dreamer, nursemaids, park attendants and a chorus of down-and-outs. The scene is a sort of Hyde Park—each visitor coming with his

---

21. C. Morgan : The Times : October 12, 1929.

or her hope, fear, lust, agony, crime or disappointment. Yet the work is essentially poetic in the tradition of Yeats and Synge. There are 4 scenes : 1. On a Spring Morning. 2. On a Summer Noon. 3. On an Autumn Evening. 4. On a Winter Night.

Says Ernest Reynolds : "The whole play is a magnificent symbolic synthesis of present-day civilization, irradiated throughout with the vision of a true poet."[22]

Life is pitched against eternity—symbolized by processions of weird shadows appearing for sometime and then disappearing into the void. Characters move like "musical phrases in counterpoints."[23] The down-and-outs in Hyde Park sing :—

> We challenge life no more, no more with our dead faith or our dead hope ;
> We carry furled the fainting flags of a dead hope and a dead faith.
> Day sings no song, neither is there room for rest beside night in her sleeping.
> We're but a sigh for a song, and a deep sigh for a drumbeat.

But to this the Dreamer replies like the Anti-Strophe in a Greek Chorus :—

> Way for the strong, and the swift and the fearless.
> Life that is stirr'd with the fear of its life, let it die ;
> Let it sink down, and pass from our vision for ever.

Let us now conclude that the Irish drama is obsessed with the tragic and the national—with a distinct preference for the supernatural, fairy and folk-lore, legends and the present Irish question : themes which lend themselves easily to a symbolic treatment. Irish drama is inspired in the first instance by the French influence of Mallarme (Yeats was a frequent visitor to the Tuesday receptions at the Paris apartments of Mallarme) and then by the Norwegian influence of Ibsen (particularly in Martyn). Symbolism in the Irish Theatre did not develop so much on the technical side as it did in France ; but it became diffused and blurred in the Celtic twilight-forging ties with the Russian and Japanese theatres.

Sometimes as in Synge, Martyn and Dunsany symbolism is organic and subtle ; but then as in Robinson and Sean O'Casey, it

22. Modern English Drama : (1949) Harrap & Co. p. 156.
23. W. Starkie in The Irish Theatre : L. Robinson 1939 : p. 175.

becomes thin and local—facing three dangers : *expressionism*(as in Toller and Kaiser in Germany and Rice, Munro and Berkeley in England), *drama of Ideas* (already in vogue under the influence of Ibsen, Galsworthy and Shaw) and finally the general English sense of *realism*-so alien to the Irish temperament but suiting the genius of Anglo-Irish dramatists like St. John Ervine.

The Irish comedy tends to farce ; tragedy to pathos. Often through local atmosphere shines out the essential human nature. To the realist artist it opens out new vistas of observation ; to the romanticist, it offers the fascination of the exotic and the weird. Irish drama has a strong tendency to Dream Play as in *Within the Gates ;* often we have to see things from the point of view of the character concerned—a sort of play within a play. Symbolism sometimes lapses into expressionism, realism and fantasy—in each case tempering with the dramatic structure of the Irish plays. But sometimes, symbolism conduces to suspension of disbelief and a rare tenseness of atmosphere as in *A Night at An Inn* and *The Lost Leader*. We agree with Percival Wilde when he asserts that only a proper context can justify the inclusion of ghosts and fairies in the play. The average reader :

> "Does not object to strange happenings in the plays which Lord Dunsany has placed outside space and nor does he object to the appearance of the angels in Yeats's "The Countess Cathleen" for the scene is laid in Ireland and in olden times. But he would protest loudly if the same angels appeared at the corner of the 42 Street, and there were no natural explanation."[24]

Both in characters and situations, there is a suggestive indefiniteness of vague and therefore, of spiritual effect. The Irish drama seems to come nearer the English notion of Fantasy, which is traceable from Shakespeare through the Romantic Poetry to the modern drama of Barrie and Masefield.

Further, the symbols used by the Irish dramatists are not fixed like the Cross, the Swastika or Stars and Stripes. They are no organic, logical and definite symbols as we find in Dante's *Divine Comedy*. At best, the symbols may be called conventional or theatrical ; they are hardly dynamic and real. Irish morality, sympathy for Lost Leaders and parricides, fairy world and angels, love of Ireland : these symbols are regressive, not progressive. To be progressive, the symbols must

---

24. The Craftsmanship of the One-act Play . 1936 p, 227.

reflect the pattern of the dramatist's ideas in their special context as in the French Symbolic poetry.

No wonder, many critics have opined that the bulk of Irish dramatic activity is a splendid failure — a tragic attempt at poetic symbolism even though unique in the simplicity of structure and diction.